JUST CALL ME SGT. MOM: A MOTHER'S JOURNEY INTO AUTISM

By Sabrina D. Guthrie

D1743196

Dedication

I dedicate this book to my dad. He went to join the Lord this year. He was truly my best friend and one of my daughter's biggest supporters. Daddy, I did it. You held my hand the whole time I worked on this project and I know you still are in my heart. I love you, daddy. You are greatly missed.

Author's Note:

I knew that diving into this project would change my life. It's not exactly the easiest task in the world to write about your life, to journal it for the whole world to see and read. I always knew that one day I wanted to transcribe my daughter's life in some fashion, to tell her story. In the aspect of material, this story was easy to write. We live in a world of Autism every day. It was also the hardest project I have ever decided to take on. Emotionally, it's not easy to lay out your feelings and desires for everyone to see. The love I have for my children is unending. They are the biggest blessings I have ever received in my life and I can only hope that I make them proud one day. If somehow, this story can affect another parent, family member, or change someone's perception of others, then I feel like I have accomplished my goal. Thank you for taking the time to share our story. Brianna's story.

Chapter 1

My Golden Girl

Brianna came into this world on January 19, 2005. She was a gorgeous baby. I realize that's a biased opinion since all parents think their children are the most beautiful creations in the world. But she was. She was my miracle.

Two weeks prior to her birth, I had to say goodbye to one of my best friends, my mother. Mom passed away unexpectedly, leaving us all in shock. It was one of the hardest goodbyes I've ever had to make, but tragedy was followed by joy. At 4:10 p.m. on the afternoon of the nineteenth, I said hello to one of the most precious miracles of all. And although my mother couldn't be there with me physically, I knew she was still there sharing the miracle with me. I'll never forget the smile my newborn shared with me the first time I held her close. I realize newborns aren't supposed to smile, and if they do it's probably gas related, but she *did* smile. That smile confirmed my belief that my mother was there with me. It's a moment I will remember for the rest of my life.

We brought Brianna home a couple of days later after she was released from the hospital and were surrounded by congratulations and hugs. There were tons of doting exclamations.

"She has the face of an angel."

"She is such a doll!"

One woman declared, "No baby is supposed to be that cute!"

Yes, I let those statements go to my head. The woman probably said that about every newborn she met, but I didn't care. I was proud. To me, no baby was cuter than my little bundle of joy.

Brianna was the best baby a mother could ask for. She rarely cried and would only do so when she was hungry or had a soiled diaper. She was easy going, and though she liked to trail me around from room to room, she was very good at entertaining herself and rarely got upset. The comments from my friends and family were always the same.

"You are so lucky!" one said.

"Is your child always that good?" another asked.

"I wish mine would entertain herself half as good as yours," one mother pointed out. Needless to say, I was one proud momma.

Maybe in hindsight, I should have noticed that Brianna's behavior was *too* good. I was a first time mother, and I hadn't been around many babies growing up. I had no idea what to expect when Brianna was born, and with the passing of my mother, I was terrified. What would I do if my baby ran a high fever? Who would I call when I needed tips on how to ease gas or diaper rashes? Who would I celebrate with over her first big moments?

I can still remember looking at Brianna while holding her that first day. My words were soft spoken. "We shall learn together, my sweet Bri. We have each other."

Those words have never been truer. We have truly traveled this journey together. She is my golden child, my miracle, my blessing, and God's very own special angel.

Chapter 2

The Diagnosis

"Was she born with it?" someone asks as I sit waiting on Brianna's name to be called in the doctor's office.

A few weeks later, I'm in line at the store when another mom looks at me fascinated. "Did she have any symptoms?" she asks upon learning Brianna is Autistic.

Questions when out in public are normal for Brianna and me, and I can't blame the people who ask. It is natural curiosity, and even at times, a little fear as they hold their own child close. I would do the same in their shoes. Often, I am asked these questions when Brianna is spinning a cup or object while making excited or unhappy noises, her eyes glued to whatever surface she is using. She's oblivious to her surroundings, oblivious to those who watch her with curiosity or dismay. She flaps her hands, jumps up and down, and occasionally screams in excitement. A jumble of noises tumble out of her as fast as they go in. It sounds like a foreign language. I wish I had all of the answers, wish I knew how to reply to every question I'm asked. But truth is, I don't.

Was she born with it? I simply don't know. She seemed like a normal, healthy baby when she was born. She progressed nicely like any other child. It wasn't until she was two years-old that I started noticing her behavior was a little odd. I'm not sure research has proven children are born with Autism. This is my own personal belief. I believe she must have had some of the traits at birth for her to develop the way she did.

It would take more than one book to tell the story of how Brianna and I have gotten to where we are today.

My main aim for *this* book is not to share every moment of her eight year life but to share my emotions and feelings, and my daughter's emotions from my perspective. I hope this journal will help those becoming acquainted with this diagnosis, and that it will help them cope with the feelings they may face.

Symptoms are the first warning signs of Autism, but they vary depending on the spectrum in which they are diagnosed. No child exhibits the same behavior in the same way.

The first warning sign with Brianna was her docile nature. She was *literally* the best baby I could have ever asked for. She was so quiet. I don't remember her crying unless she was hungry or wet. Nothing seemed to bother her. She was easily entertained even as an infant. All movement fascinated her, captivating her for hours at a time. Her even temper was often complimented. Though I suspect her docile behavior was a sign of Autism (and have often read it is), it may not have been a symptom at all. Many babies are amazingly good in the early years.

Brianna was my first child, so I tend to beat myself up for not noticing the signs sooner. At checkups, doctors assured me she was progressing beautifully so I never considered that something might be wrong. She developed some language early on, saying words like "momma" and "daddy", but never developed a full vocabulary. By the time she was two years-old, her speech was limited. She would sing verses to different songs but she didn't converse. She never asked for me. In fact, she only said momma and daddy when prompted. Never on her own. She would follow me around the house and point and gesture to the things she wanted or needed.

Warning bells rang in my head but the doctors still

seemed unfazed, and I was drowning in denial. There couldn't be anything wrong with my gorgeous, precious angel. I shrugged off her speech issues and attributed it to the fact that she wasn't around many kids her age. My ex-husband was in the military and only a handful of our friends had children.

Watching my baby girl play made my heart clench. I was scared to admit it, but there was obviously something wrong. It was a hard thing to face after my mother's death and my failing marriage. But denial lasts only so long before realization dawns. What was once attributed to something else could no longer be explained away.

My second child, Charlie, was born eighteen months after Brianna. It was his birth that challenged my denial. Charlie developed quickly, speaking earlier and hitting milestones twice as fast as his sister. During routine and sick visits, I began asking doctors about Brianna's development. Brianna was having bad ear infections and we were visiting the doctor frequently. The only answers I received were quizzical brows and shaking heads. Her lack of speech didn't concern them. I was told allergies and the accompanying ear infections were hindering her speech development. They attacked the infections with antibiotics and sent us on our way.

After a year at home, I went back to work. Daycare workers picked up on Brianna's behavior early on. One employee pointed out her lack of interest in other children. She was perfectly content being alone and would play quietly until I picked her up after work. Charlie, on the other hand, was a social butterfly. My frustrations and fear grew. My world revolved around my children.

My mother-in-law was the first person to mention the word Autism. It was honestly the first time I'd ever heard of the disorder. The thought terrified me. I shrugged off my mother-in-law's remark, but her words stayed with me. I began to research Autism. The symptoms I found made my hands shake. So many of them reminded me of Brianna; the lack of social skills, loss or lack of speech, and little eye contact. There were other symptoms but I ignored them because Brianna hadn't exhibited those. It was because of these "other" symptoms that I clung to my denial. Maybe, just maybe, Brianna didn't have autism. Maybe my mother-in-law was wrong. Maybe Brianna was just slower, more delayed than her brother.

Upon closer research, I discovered that no child in the autism spectrum was the same. Even those with similar symptoms were different. My heart sank.

I moved home a few months later to Mississippi to be closer to my family. As a single parent, I worked full time. Life was chaotic but good.

I took Brianna for her first appointment with her new pediatrician, and I was impressed She listened to my concerns and worked to help me narrow down the cause of Brianna's delays. We saw an ENT to clear up the ear infections we'd been battling since she was two. She needed tubes. The infections had left her with almost ninety percent hearing loss. I was shocked the doctors I'd seen before hadn't caught any of this. I take my children to the doctor at the earliest signs of sickness. They sneeze, I schedule an appointment. I admit, I'm an overprotective parent. I often wonder if the doctors just got tired of listening to my questions. Getting a new set of doctors was the best thing that ever happened to us.

A few weeks after her initial visit, Brianna had surgery. The doctor was amazed at the infection he had to clear out. Apparently, Brianna's body had become accustomed to the onslaught of antibiotics, and the medicines were no longer helping. The surgery produced immediate results. She could hear! It was an amazing sight to behold. Her eyes grew wide at the smallest noises. Watching her rediscover the world brought tears to my eyes. Her daycare teachers saw an improvement. Brianna danced around the room after hearing music played in the classroom. I cried tears of joy.

I felt more at ease. It wasn't autism, right? Maybe *this* was the problem. Maybe I hadn't fought hard enough with the doctors to heal her ears. Maybe it was my fault her development was so slow. I beat myself up pretty badly. Guilt swamped me as I watched her react to new sounds.

But as Brianna's hearing cleared, her odd behaviors increased. Music and other specific sounds were soon becoming Brianna's favorite noises. She tested the music, using her tongue to create her own version of the sound. Even now, Brianna constantly makes sounds. Unless sleeping, she is experimenting with some type of noise; humming, clucking her tongue, or chirping.

Then the spinning began. For hours, she twirled. At first, she only twirled her body, but then she transferred this habit to objects. She can make almost anything spin. She often takes objects apart until she gets the momentum she wants out of it. Once, while attending a birthday party for a friend's little boy, Brianna silenced an entire room of four and five year-old children by spinning mini play dough cups on a table in perfect circles. Brianna was oblivious to her audience. That day, without even realizing it, she was the star of the show.

The odd behaviors and the continued speech delays were the fundamental reasons I reached out once more to doctors. Meeting with the pediatrician this time was different. There were no hearing barriers. The doctor knew something was wrong. She examined her, silently observing her, her head bobbing. She looked at me and smiled. *Smiled.* That was a good sign, right? But the smile was wrong, *forced.* I didn't receive a diagnosis that day. Instead, I was referred to the Children's Hospital in Jackson, Mississippi for further evaluation.

The first visit to Jackson led to months of doctor's visits with different specialists and clinics. We saw doctors specializing in genetics, psychology, child development, and more. The list goes on. The first diagnosis we received was Angelman's Syndrome. She had a mutation in her UBE3A gene that was associated with Angelman's, but research proved Brianna didn't fully fit all of the symptoms. They drew my blood and discovered the same mutation which ruled out that diagnosis. It was a lengthy process that wore on me and Brianna.

Our visit with the psychologist was the first step toward our autism diagnosis. Brianna's evaluation was emotionally hard to watch. She couldn't follow or understand the simplest directions. At times, I wanted to take her and leave. I was helpless. I couldn't help her, and it was killing me. Not long after that, Brianna was diagnosed. I even received a packet in the mail with the words *Developmentally Delayed and Autism* scrawled across the first page.

My heart sank. My gut hurt, my stomach a punching bag of emotions. Please understand this is an initial reaction. My heart broke, but I didn't love my baby girl any less. I was afraid for her. It didn't bother me that my child wasn't 'normal'. It was the unknown that scared me. What did the future hold? Would she ever be able to have a conversation with me? Would she ever call my

name? Would she ever be able to tell me she loved me?
Could she ever be independent? The questions were
endless. I sat in the middle of the room and cried. The
tears wouldn't stop coming. Brianna hopped into the
room, her hands flapping, her body twirling. Walking
over to me, she sat in my lap and hugged me while
waving, chirping, and singing. Brianna's eye contact
isn't bad for a child on the spectrum and she stared at me.
It wasn't long before she was off again, spinning and
chirping, but that moment was enough. It was enough to
stop the tears. It was enough to make me smile. She
wasn't doing this alone. We were in this together.

Chapter 3

Research and Planning

Where do we go next? What do we do now? Too many questions, too many answers from doctors who didn't always know. Her main doctor gave me recommendations for speech therapy and a jump start program with the school system and sent me on my way. It was left up to me at that point. We followed the recommendations to the letter. I signed her up for the program at school and we started speech therapy at the wellness center in our area. No other therapies were mentioned. I felt like Brianna and I were paddling along a slow moving river with only one oar. I turned to what I knew best … books and the internet.

There isn't much I haven't read about Autism and the treatments available. Technically, there is no cure. I've read about children who seem fully cured by a technique, diet, or some other medical intervention. Whether they are actually cured or remain so is not always clear. It's amazing how many suggestions, therapies, and homeopathic remedies are out there boasting about their ability to help Autism. I explored them all eagerly. I made huge lists, my excitement growing with each new attempt to scale the Autism wall. It didn't take long for the glamour to fade.

For one thing, no one tells you going into all of this stuff just how expensive it is to try these innovative ideas, and insurance rarely covers experimental treatment. All of the testimonials from parents raving about how this approach cured their child or helped their child become normal were great until shopping around revealed the price tag on these approaches … financially and emotionally. For a middle class family depending on each paycheck, this was extremely discouraging. I often wish I could win the lottery, just so I could have the finances available to be able to give my daughter all the help that I would like to get her. In reality, one approach at a time was all that we could financially manage and some of them weren't even possible at all. It was staggering. It depressed me.

The controversial question loomed: Do I want to find a cure if one is available? This is where the emotions come in. Truly, I'm human. I would absolutely love to have my daughter walk up to me and say, "Mommy, I love you. I had a great day today." I often find myself watching her as she spins her new favorite toy, her tongue clucking. And I ask myself, *What's going through her head?* Selfishly, I cry. Why can't I just walk up to my little girl and have a conversation? Why can't I ask her a question and get an answer? Why can't I ask her what's hurting so I can help her when she's sick instead of making guesses? Why can't I find the cause of her frustrations before a meltdown occurs?

Here's the answer. God gave me a special child. He knew that she would make a difference in this world, whether it be within our family or to thousands of others. I thank God everyday for trusting me with such a special gift. Autistic children are so intelligent. I've been blessed to see glimpses of Brianna's intellect on many occasions. Would I change that part? Never. I love how she is able to decipher the world in a way I could never comprehend. Would I want a cure? Yes. Not in the way she thinks. I know there are thousands of ideas and new discoveries created from genius minds, minds like Brianna's and other children like her. But if I was given a tool or the ability to knock down the wall in Brianna's mind that allows her to communicate, I would do it in a heartbeat. To be able to look at her, our eyes connecting—*truly* connecting—as she asks me something simple such as, "Would it be okay to watch tv?" I would love that. But for now, I'll take all the hugs I can get. I'll take the gestures and words that she is able to give me. I will never take those for granted. In retrospect, there are some things I would cure and some things I would leave alone. It's said Albert Einstein was a genius. Why mess with intelligence?

I won't detail every therapy or homeopathic remedy that we have tried. There is a list. We have tried the GFCF diet, many vitamins, and clay baths. We have tried probiotics, as these aid in removing overgrowth of yeast. According to online sources, yeast can cause an increase in symptoms in Autistic children. We did see differences, albeit small ones, with some of these treatments but never substantial. So far, our best attempts at normalcy have been school and therapy. We have an amazing teacher and group of therapists.

Where do I go from here? To the next book or research that I can lay my hands on. Because as her mother, I know that I am also her doctor, her teacher, and her friend. She relies on me to lead the way. Do I get frustrated because we haven't met all the goals that I've set in my mind? Yes. Not because I want her to be normal. No, it's because I worry about what will happen to her when something happens to me. Right now, she depends on me fully. My dreams have changed over the years. My goals for her are still high and always will be because I strive for the highest possible dreams for all my kids including Brianna. But my goals are changing, going from technical to realistic. How do I help Brianna achieve a degree of independence?

My main goal is to see her grow into a young lady capable of having some form of independence. Right now she needs assistance for pretty much everything: dressing, eating, bathing, using the potty, the list goes on. If I could just have the chance to see my little girl be able to do some of these things for herself, I would feel a million times better about having to say goodbye to her one day. I can only hope that the good Lord above will allow me to witness some of these things before he takes me home.

Chapter 4

The Mommy Zombie

No one could have prepared me for the challenges of raising a child on the spectrum. No one can prepare you to be a parent to a normal child, let alone a child with a disability. No self help book or magazine, no matter how much advice is given, can prepare you for the daily trials ahead. Every child is different.

When Brianna was diagnosed, I had several roads to travel: denial, self-pity, heart ache, shame, guilt, confusion, and especially fear. I was scared. Truly terrified. I had absolutely no idea what I was doing. Five years later and I'm still scared and completely lost. I've never been good with directions. We take each day as it comes.

No one prepared me for one particular obstacle: sleep. I read somewhere that kids with Autism don't need as much sleep as most people. Where I read this, I have no idea. I simply cannot remember, but it is one aspect of my life that has changed drastically since I brought my daughter into this world.

Sleep, such a beautiful, relaxing word. It's become a foreign concept, a word that Brianna has no use for, or didn't for a very long time. Her sleep schedule, even as a baby, was odd and complicated. She never followed a pattern. I never knew when she would be awake. I know that's pretty normal for an infant. The beauty of a first child before the siblings follow is simple. When she slept, I slept. It was an easy enough solution. When my son was born, however, I began to realize quickly that sleep would soon be a distant memory.

After Brianna's diagnosis, her lack of sleep—and mine—increased. It increased so much; it was almost as if her body was telling her it didn't need sleep at all. I kid you not, when I say that we honestly went weeks at a time with only a few hours of sleep. I think we even went one whole week with only ten hours devoted to slumber. I was in tears. I was working a full time schedule at work while staying up with a little girl that giggled and played all night long. We may have gotten two to three hours of sleep a night and that was *only* if I was lucky.

I called and made an appointment with her doctor. I'm pretty sure I was early to that appointment. I didn't even give the pediatrician a chance to say hello before I was on her like mayonnaise to bread with tons of questions about sleep cycles and how to make her body understand that it needed rest. Thankfully, we have a very understanding doctor and she gave me a reassuring smile. Then she wrote down a name, a common vitamin that became my salvation: Melantonin. I'm sure every person in the pharmacy that day thought I was a crazy lunatic with the dark circles under my eyes and a huge Coca-cola in my hand as I browsed the vitamin aisle. I'm pretty sure my hair was a mess, and if I wore makeup, it was probably done wrong. I quickly grabbed the melatonin and made my way home hoping for a night of rest.

I noticed a change immediately. She took the smallest dose suggested, but that was all it took. I gave it to her an hour before bedtime and about thirty minutes later, she slowly drifted off to sleep. I began implementing as much bedtime routine as possible during those thirty minutes to help her understand that bedtime was a necessary part of life. It took a long time and a lot of sleepless hours to get her into a definite routine but we managed with many prayers and help from up above.

Today, we no longer use the Melantonin. The bedtime routine seems to be enough for her. She will even come and get me when she knows it's time to be tucked in. Have we completely sidestepped the no sleep scenario? Not a chance. She is still a very early riser and there are nights here and there that we repeat the days from old, but we are at a much better place than before and those extra hours make all the difference!

Chapter 5

The Meltdowns

"What do you find most challenging?" I have to admit that this question when asked is the easiest for me to answer. Meltdowns are common in most Autistic children. Overstimulation, communication barriers, and other triggers can result in long and exhaustive hair raising fits of frustration. Like all children, Brianna will sometimes throw a good old fashioned tantrum when circumstances don't always go her way, but I can usually tell the difference between the meltdowns and the latter.

Meltdowns occur when I least expect them. One moment she will be okay and the next, you would think you were watching the movie The Exorcist. Loud screaming, uncontrollable tears, and worst of all, the pain she tries to inflict upon herself. She bangs her head and often hits herself on the chin. These meltdowns can occur anytime and anyplace. Too many people in a crowded area causing overstimulation of her senses, communication barriers, illness, headaches, and several other situations can cause them to appear at a moment's notice. It brings new meaning to the story Dr. Jekyll and Mr. Hyde.

The first meltdowns I ever experienced happened when she was only two years old. They came at night in her sleep. It was enough to make the hair stand up on my arms. I would awake to a blood curdling scream that would send me flying into her room to find her thrashing around in the bed, eyes closed, screaming at the top of her lungs. I would try everything in my power to get those screams to stop by trying, sometimes unsuccessfully, to arouse her from her slumber or lying down next to her and talking to her softly. These would happen frequently, sometimes nightly. I spent many hours silently helping her fight the demons in the night, many times with us both falling back to sleep after shedding many tears between the two of us.

I was terrified. It was my first glimpse, my first inkling that something was wrong. Something wasn't right. We fought the night terrors for several months and then one morning, we woke up and they were gone. Just disappeared and never returned. It was almost as if they never existed. However, the memories have never left me. I still get emotional thinking of those nights, not knowing how to ease my daughter's pain. Doctor's really had no answers for me then, just suggestions and advice that never worked.

A little over a year later, Brianna was diagnosed with Autism and Developmentally Delayed. The meltdowns moved from night to daytime. To begin with the meltdowns could last for hours. I would be in tears and crumpled on the floor with her before I would realize the cause so I could help comfort her.

Going out in public became a challenge because I didn't yet know which situations would trigger the worst episodes. I remember once eating in a restaurant with my sister and brother-in-law. We picked the worst time ever to go out and eat. Church had just released and everyone was coming in to eat after morning services. We are from the South and reside in the Bible Belt so you can imagine just how many folks that warranted. There were a lot and Brianna's senses became terribly over stimulated. I could see the fear in her eyes before the meltdown occurred and my stomach tightened in response. It wasn't long before she planted her small body underneath the table while holding on to the pole underneath like it was her only life line. The cries that emanated from her were loud enough to catch the attention of everyone in the room. People stopped placing orders and silence reigned.

I looked at my sister frantically as I tried my hardest to peel her small hands off the pole so I could get her outside. She wasn't budging and for a three year-old she was amazingly strong when she became frightened. My brother-in-law became the hero that day as he leaned down and helped me move her fingers little by little from the pole. He picked her up quickly and jogged for the exit while my sister and I grabbed the other kids and ran out behind him. It didn't take long for the fresh air outside to help ease Brianna's screams away and everyone inside went from freeze mode back to mobile again. It was almost as if someone had paused a movie and started it back as soon as we exited.

Over the years, I've gotten better at reading my daughter. Watching all the signs allowed me to diffuse the meltdowns early causing them to be short lived and less exhaustive. Most of her meltdowns now are cut in half lasting thirty minutes at the most. Sometimes we are even lucky enough to make it an entire day without any incidents.

I have become in tune to my daughter's needs so much so, that there are times when I feel as if we are of one body instead of two. Scouting out her needs before my own has become second nature. I feel like a detective on a crime show. Before we even walk out the door, I've already calculated the dangers, the situations and type of meltdowns some situations may induce. I plan for the worst and investigate all escape routes. I'm a small person, only 5'1 in height. Brianna is a big girl and can already fit into most of my clothing. She is already to the point where she can overpower me. So I stay a step ahead. I prepare for what might come.

I'm grateful on one account. Brianna has a loving heart. Despite her problems with communication, she loves to hug and give kisses. She loves attention. Although she has the tendency to hurt herself when in meltdown mode, she has never hurt those around her.

Why are the meltdowns most challenging to handle? Simply put, it's hard to watch. It's hard to see your child so frustrated that she would want to cause herself harm. It's hard to see her hurting and not knowing what's causing the pain. It's hard to see that deer in headlights look in her eyes when she's in a situation where she's over stimulated. It's heartbreaking. I find myself crying myself to sleep after a hard day of continuous fits. I wish I could get inside her head and see what's causing all her frustrations and pain. If I had the ability, I'd switch places with her in a heartbeat. Take all of it away. Unfortunately, my super hero powers don't extend that far. I made a promise to Brianna a long time ago, during those first few night terrors and I will keep that promise. I promised that I would help her fight, help her succeed where she is weak. I promised to catch her when she falls and help her move forward, and I promised that we would do this together. I won't let her fight this world of hers alone.

Chapter 6

Who Needs Hollywood?

"Wow, look at that," one woman says as Brianna hits the floor in a huge succession of screams and fits.

"That child needs a good spanking!" another man says as he passes me in the parking lot.

"What's wrong with her?" a child asks her parents as she watches Brianna flap her hands, a mix of happy and mad noises streaming from her mouth.

"Oh you poor thing, you have your hands full," an older woman says while patting me on the back.

We never go anywhere without an audience, flying remarks, sympathetic stares, and sometimes even looks of disgust. We've even cleared out waiting rooms at doctors' offices because parents are afraid for their child to be near mine. It was easier in Brianna's younger years to pass off some of Brianna's odd behaviors on being a toddler. As she continues to grow, it's become more and more apparent she doesn't fit in with the "norm" of today's society.

Fitting in has never bothered me much as a parent. Growing up, I was always too shy, too awkward, too quiet, too pimply, and all around too geeky, my nose always in a book. I never really liked the term, "fitting in". What does that really mean anyway? Fitting in meant more peer pressure and a busier schedule than I already had. I was comfortable with my every day routine. I had a few close friends, my family, and as I got older and less awkward, even a small string of boyfriends. Popularity is exhausting, even lonely. I've always been much happier being myself. I'm pretty happy with who I am, and as a parent, I want my kids to feel the same way. I want them to be proud of who they are.

I am proud of all three of my beautiful children. I'm proud of Brianna. I'm proud that she likes to sing her noises to the world, that she likes to collect watering cans in every shape and color, and that she thinks spinning and making objects fly are cool. Because underneath all of those odd behaviors, I see a child that has an amazing intellect, a child that loves to laugh, a child that has more bravery than I will ever have in a lifetime.

Do you ever get embarrassed? Yes. It's hard to say but true. One of the hardest parts of deciding to write this book, to share my thoughts and feelings on raising a child on the spectrum, was to be completely honest. I'm human, and I would be lying if I said I never got embarrassed during the tougher, more horrifying meltdowns. I beat myself up the first few times the meltdowns happened in town. I would get overwhelmed and embarrassed, tears streaming down my cheeks as I carried a then small Brianna to the car. For a long time afterward, I would cry, ashamed of myself for being embarrassed of my child. But as Brianna grew and time passed, I realized there wasn't a reason to be ashamed. But there also wasn't a reason to be ashamed of being embarrassed.

Embarrassment is a common emotion and no one should be ashamed for feeling it. The true importance lies in how I handle it. As a child, and even as an adult, I suffer from shyness. You know the "imagine everyone in their underwear" concept? I've done that. And now, I simply make people disappear.

Does it always work? Not always. Hurtful remarks and unabashed stares at the checkout counter during meltdowns still hurt, still make my face burn and my body go numb. The impatient cursing from people behind me in line still stings. But the only thing I can do is smile and shrug. I disappear into a world where only my kids and I exist. I tune out all the noises around me and I concentrate on diffusing the problem. Tunnel vision has become my best friend.

I'm like the sweating bomb squad officer on one of those TV shows, the one frantically trying to disable a bomb before the whole building blows except I'm diffusing the bomb going off in my child's brain. I'm trying to figure out what is causing her overstimulation or anxiety, so that I can quickly disable it.

It's all about routine now. I time our outings by time of day. I know that in the mornings and early afternoon, Brianna is going to be in a much better mood than in the latter part of the day. By nightfall, her brain has already entered overdrive from all the stimulates that she's dealt with from the morning. If I need to run an errand or make a shopping trip, I schedule it early in the day.

Do the comments and actions of others hurt? Yes, I would be lying if I said that cruelty from others doesn't sting because it does. I don't let it bother me as a person because the older Brianna gets, the more used to the reactions I become. I worry mostly about Brianna. It's the mama bear mentality. I'm never ugly during a confrontation. If anything, I just hope I teach people about our situation. I look at them and say, "This is my daughter and I love her. She has Autism, is mostly nonverbal, and although she's a little overwhelmed right now, she's nowhere near stupid and she understands a lot of the remarks that you are saying so I ask kindly that you take them elsewhere."

I can't get inside Brianna's brain. I don't know how much of what Brianna hears makes sense to her, what she understands. I do know that when I ask her to do something, she shows me she understands by doing it. And although it's rare, there have been times when I've gotten a simple "yes" or "no" response. So in retrospect, I know she's got to understand some of the hurtful remarks and that tears me up inside. They can say all the unkind things in the world to me but I don't want Brianna to feel like she's unwanted or a freak.

Are all people like this? No. I've met some amazing people, people who have offered assistance, who have offered a shoulder to cry on, and an ear when I needed to talk. It's a diverse world. The good truly does balance the evil.

I don't see an end to meltdowns anytime soon in our future. We may never see an end to them, and I've accepted that. That doesn't mean I won't work toward a day where she might have more independence and have the ability to speak more. Until then, I have my bomb squad equipment ready, and I will continue to work on diffusing the problem.

Chapter 7

Potty Training is the Devil

Really, what parent doesn't groan at the mention of potty training? Who doesn't get frustrated? I have a son that has already gone through it and a two year-old that is *still* going through it. Then there is Brianna. I am a godly, Christian woman so please don't judge me when I say this, but we have honestly been through potty training hell for the last six years. Each year, I just know it's going to be the year. Each year, I get suited up, geared up, and wave my hand in the air declaring that we are going to reach this timeless goal. At the end of each year, I smile through clenched, determined teeth and say, "we always have next year."

I'm convinced at this point that she knows the mechanisms of using the toilet. She can sit on it, flush it, wash her hands, and all the other necessary actions like a champ. She just won't *use* it. She makes loud noises (her form of curse words I'm sure) at the mere mention of 'potty'. She's stubborn, my Brianna. My dad would be the first one to tell you she gets it honestly.

She has found ways to communicate to let me know she's gone "stinky" and that indicates to me that she's ready to use the restroom. I have tried every approach from picture boards, movies, timed sitting periods, and other techniques I have read and researched. It has all ended with very little luck and lots and lots of meltdowns. I have finally come to one conclusion: she simply doesn't want to use it. The potty either scares her or she simply just doesn't like it. It doesn't fit into her world.

I wish she could tell me why she doesn't want to use the potty so that I have an idea where I keep going wrong. I know Brianna understands a lot of what I tell her. I talk to her as much as I can. I've broached the potty topic, but she answers me with screams and blank stares. Google "potty training" on the web and you will find tons of tips, advice, and interesting stories. I have enough horror stories to build a bridge to the South Pacific.

I never intended for potty training to be a large part of this story. Sharing my experiences in this area seems more private, especially when dealing with an older child. Hopefully, sharing my frustrations will help parents dealing with the same situation to feel better, to know you are not alone. My best friend and I were sitting on the porch one morning drinking coffee and discussing our children and she looked at me and said, "I think she'll just surprise you one day and start going. She'll use it on Brianna's time." Honestly, she is probably right. Brianna has a way of doing things on her time. Until then, we will continue to keep trying all the approaches we can and pray that one day she surprises us. I'll keep my party hat safely tucked away and we will be ready to celebrate in a big way.

Chapter 8

The Patience of Job

This was always one of my most favorite stories in the Bible. Crazy, right? How could a story about a man that is pretty much tortured by the devil to prove his devotion to God be a favorite Bible story? It's not the horrific trials that Job endured that makes this story one of my favorites, it's his continuous and unfailing love in his creator that makes it such a timeless story.

Someone once told me that I had the patience of Job. She said she would never in a million years be able to do the things I do with Brianna on a daily basis. I smiled politely and nodded, but I disagree. Job didn't technically have patience. He had faith, a faith so strong that no matter how many trials he endured, no matter how frustrated he became, he still knew in his heart that God would deliver him from the devil's hands.

Faith. That's the word I prefer to hear over anything else. I have faith that my daughter will one day be able to do the things I so desperately want her to do to gain some type of independence. I have faith that even if she never progresses past the point she's at now that the Lord still has big plans for my beautiful angel. Maybe it's his plan for her to teach the world about Autism, about the huge spectrum that exists out there. Maybe it's to give us another special angel in this world to love and care for. And maybe she has been put here simply to touch lives, to show people the world through her eyes.

In reality, I have very little patience. I'm not at all a patient person. I've never been good at waiting and I get frustrated easily. I'm a normal true blooded mother like any mother. I lose my cool from time to time, I cry when

I get overwhelmed, and I even admit to the occasional mommy temper tantrum. *Mommy temper tantrum?* You know those days where the kids love to team up on you. While changing a diaper, one decides that a permanent marker makes great wall art and another decides that my phone looks better in the toilet. Yep, those are tantrum moments. It usually involves a quick count to ten and a mommy time out.

Mommy time out? Mommy time outs are necessary from time to time because I know that if they didn't exist I would probably have to be institutionalized. Time outs require a room with a lock so that when three huge messes occur at the exact same time, I can hide for a few minutes to gather my wits, to release some of the anger. I am convinced that my children strategically schedule these episodes to test my endurance. We shall call it the mommy boot camp.

Mommy boot camp? Mommy boot camps are technically my children's way of testing how far they can go when it comes to messes and play without making mommy go completely loco. I picture my children in military fatigues as they prep me for these "moments" to test how I will handle each one. The terrible twos, for example, is a boot camp all on its own. With triumph, I fist pump and celebrate while dragging my battered, bruised, and wore out body through each figurative graduation.

I'm not ashamed to admit I've hidden in that room and locked the door while two sets of hands knock and yell mommy as Brianna makes her happy noises in the background. She's always content with the mess she's created, which normally involves a container and some water. I count to ten. Little fingers slide underneath the door and wiggle followed by giggles. I count to ten again. I feel more confident. The battle plan is set.

There are whispers on the other side of the door, more childish plotting. One final breath, and I'm ready to face it. I open the door and say their names, their full names, and watch in satisfaction as they turn around to face me, their eyes wide. A calm mom is even scarier than an angry one. Mommy is calm which means mommy is also ready to dole out punishment. My two year-old squeals, and each child runs except Brianna who still thinks her mess was the work of genius. But I'm faster, bigger, and as they turn to run, I'm in front of them with a smile on my face and my hands on my hips. Two faces pout, and I know I've once again graduated to the next level.

And then there are the days where the autism is the hardest to face. The days where meltdowns are endless, starting in the morning and not ending until bedtime. Those are the days where Brianna's communication wall is hard to scale. Usually, she's sick and unable to tell me she feels bad. Those days are painstakingly long. My other two children usually break down with her because they don't understand the screaming. They don't understand what upsets her, and they become frustrated because mommy's attention is focused on calming the screams and not on them. They whine and fuss like any normal child would when feeling ignored. Brianna picks up on their unhappiness and screams and cries louder. Those are the days we usually fall asleep deflated and exhausted, drying tears on our cheeks. Thankfully, those days don't happen near as often as they used to, and when they do, I say a few extra prayers for strength and endurance.

Patience plays a very small role. Faith. I have faith that I can wake up each day and take each moment as it comes. I have faith that I can fight the good fight, and even when I lose, still lose with a smile on my face and the knowledge that there is a nice soft bed waiting for me at the end of each day. I have faith that no matter how many messes I have to clean up, how many cries I have to soothe, how many injuries I have to doctor, and no matter how many walls of communication with Brianna I have to climb, at the end of each day there are still hugs and "I loves you's" waiting for me as I tuck them safely into bed each night. I have faith in my love for them. It will never dissipate. It always grows.

Chapter 9

The Hermit...Social outcast?

"She didn't show up today. She said she would come."

I imagine that's what some friends say when we don't always show up for parties or events. I can't tell you how bad I feel, how *guilty,* for not showing up to a place that I RSVP. I'll be honest. I hate invitations that RSVP. Why? I understand the need for a head count. I do. But one thing I've learned about raising a child with autism is that I can't make promises. I never know what each day will bring, what obstacles we'll face. And then there are those times when I'm simply exhausted. The day before may have been a tough one. I may have been up most of the night dealing with meltdowns and extra clean ups.

I think most parents with a child with special needs will tell you that each day is a challenge. Each day brings new changes and new discoveries. A large majority of my friends do not have children with special needs, but thankfully, most of them understand. I know some don't and that's okay. I don't expect them too. Writing a journal is the same as baring your soul. There is nothing more inspiring to me than raising a child on the spectrum, but in doing so; I also have to admit things I don't like admitting even to myself.

One admission: I hate birthday parties. That sounds horrible, right? Why? They are exhausting, and there have often been more times than not when we've had to leave because of a major meltdown. One such party resulted in my brother-in-law having to carry Brianna out after an explosive meltdown over a cupcake. Thankfully, this party was thrown by my best friend and her family was very understanding.

Brianna has a huge obsession with food. It's a battle we struggle with everyday. It's the main reason we have the majority of our meltdowns. In fact, it is one of the reasons why we will be visiting genetics doctors and clinics in the next few months. It's to rule out a disorder that centers on food. Brianna's body doesn't seem to understand that it's full. She could literally eat herself to death. I wish I was kidding about that, but I'm not. We have found her eating out of butter dishes from the refrigerator or throwing up because she got into a box of cookies. We have wrestled many times over a piece of food just to end up crying together in the middle of the floor. Her, because she doesn't understand why she can't continuously eat. Me, because I feel powerless to help her to understand it.

Brianna does fight a battle with weight, and she is obese. I feel a huge amount of blame for that because in the early years we would use food to reward her, using it for positive reinforcement. After her uphill weight gain, we switched to toys as a reward, but her fight with food continues. I admit there are days I give in. I let her have that extra piece of candy or food after battling continuous meltdowns. I hate myself for that. I hate myself daily for those moments of weakness. As she gets older, I'm getting stronger and better at saying no but the battle still rages every day.

This brings me back to the birthday party. Birthday parties have cakes and other goodies that Brianna gravitates too immediately. How do you explain to people that your daughter has a problem with food and doesn't understand that she can't just run to the cake and dig in? Trust me, she has done this on several occasions, and has at times, succeeded. The disgust I see on people's faces when it happens destroys me. How do you ask parents to please hide the cake until it's time to serve it, especially when money has been spent and parents want it proudly displayed. You just can't do that. Thankfully, my family and closest friends know this, and they usually design their parties to avoid the meltdowns. But to ask that of everyone would be unkind.

So I admit I sometimes make excuses when parties come up. I hide, so I don't have to hear the screams and cries when I have to tell Brianna no. I avoid the situation altogether. Do I get shunned for it? Maybe. I can only hope for understanding and forgiveness. I am, after all, human.

Do we avoid going out altogether? No, we love taking our kids places and doing things with them. I do tend to avoid places and parties that serve large amounts of food because I know she'll try and binge eat until she's sick and my heart can't handle that.

Brianna's favorite attractions are aquariums. She loves them, and I have taken her to several over the years. Something about watching the fish in the tanks and looking at all the lights and water fascinate her. We usually stay in them for hours at a time. And thankfully, it's a trip that is enjoyed by all the kids and not just her.

Water parks are another attraction that we avoid like the plague. We have tried a few times but after Brianna shoved several people out of the way and had some extremely bad meltdowns when she couldn't understand that she had to wait in line, we decided it wasn't for us. Going to a creek or pool is much better on all of us and more enjoyable.

So I guess you can say, we pick and choose what suits us all, where we can all have the best time with less stress and less meltdowns. We strategically plan each outing. Does that always work? No, but we learn from each experience. We keep a mental checklist of the activities that work, the ones we all enjoy and those that just don't work at all.

Chapter 10

Extra Extra...Mommy's Going Out!

There's nothing better in this world than becoming a parent. Even as a little girl, I dreamed of being a mommy. I've always known I wanted children and each one of mine has been a true blessing. Does that mean I don't get stressed, that I don't have the occasional break down? Definitely not.

Those stressed out moments are the main reason why I try and plan a night out at least every other month or every few months. I seldom ask for a babysitter. I just don't really have the need for one, but every once in a while, I cave. Thankfully, I have my sisters, Mamaw, Nana, and Grandma to offer a hand when I need that time out. Usually, I schedule a few hours out with a friend or Kevin to see a movie or go to dinner. Those few hours mean more to me than a full night off. Those hours allow me to relax, to rebuild my stamina, to return home recharged. My kids look forward to it because they know mommy will come home refreshed and ready for another day. I don't feel guilty for those simple escapes. Sometimes, when the stress builds up, it's okay to take a deep breath and go for coffee. I think it's that ability to know when you need to step back a moment that makes a better parent.

The same goes for my two non-autistic children. I know they often feel cheated because they can't always do what other kids do because of Brianna. For example, Charlie loves to go to the movies, but with Brianna it's impossible. I've learned it's okay to get a sitter or call one of my sisters to plan that time for him. I want them to know they can have their recharging moment too.

Everyone deserves a chance to relax, even if it's as simple as reading a book. Even Brianna needs them. I often take her to do things she enjoys that her siblings either don't enjoy or don't understand. It's her chance to be unique and recharge.

Chapter 11

Doctors, Diets, and Meds....Oh My!

This chapter title is pretty much self-explanatory. All parents that have children with any kind of disability or illness can relate to the endless hours spent inside waiting rooms. Brianna was diagnosed at the age of three, and the doctors' visits that led to diagnosis were numerous.

The first time we were sent to Jackson to the children's hospital was overwhelming. I was scared because I was pretty much being told by my regular pediatrician that something wasn't right with my little girl. A visit with the doctor in Jackson, and an evaluation later, and the pediatrician's concerns were validated. There was something wrong. Then the visits began at the Genetics clinic. These visits were endless rounds of blood samples and long hours spent in waiting rooms with a tired little girl and extra meltdowns.

There was the possible Angelman's diagnosis, later discarded, followed by an MRI that showed up normal. After that, an EEG was run. Weeks and months went by with a visit to Jackson every couple of weeks. Brianna was exhausted, my place of employment was getting irritated with the number of days I had to miss, and the stress was piling up. I dreaded waiting rooms because no matter how much I prepared for them (snack and toys), Brianna would still meltdown after so many hours. I would wake up tired before we even hit the road to make the two hour drive to the hospital for each appointment.

The tears and the fear in Brianna's eyes made the visits even worse. I hated the fear as they fought her for yet another test. She became a fighter. She struggled, and after a while, it would take a roomful of nurses to hold her down. She would have been a great contender for the UFC. I can't tell you how many times I've heard a nurse or doctor comment, "Man, she's a strong little girl." I looked at them with a sad smile and replied, "She's had to learn to be."

On many trips home, she would pass out from exhaustion and I would look at my daddy with tears on my cheeks. I don't know how I would have survived some of those trips without my dad riding with me for moral support. One of the hardest things for me to deal with emotionally was watching people hold her down as they performed another test. She would look at me from the corner of the room, her eyes full of confusion and fear. How do I explain to my little girl that what they're doing is to help her? I've cried myself to sleep over those looks. She's older now, but I still have a hard time dealing with it. She's gotten stronger and the number of people it takes to hold her down has increased. For some appointments, they now have to put her to sleep just to be able to work with her.

I wasn't shocked when we finally got a diagnosis. Autism had been suggested, and we were somewhat prepared, but it's still devastating. Please don't take that statement the wrong way. It wasn't an "end of the world" devastation. It was an "I don't want my child to have to endure this" devastation. According to the doctors, Brianna was low functioning and they had no idea how much she would develop. I'm not a quitter. I will fight for her.

But this is where the system seemed to fail. We were told a few things that we could do (such as speech therapy) and were sent home with a paper that said we would come for regular checkups every six months. That was it. After all of the hours and tears spent in every waiting room imaginable, we were sent home with literally nothing. That was the most devastating part of all.

So I went to work. I had her signed up for speech therapy twice a week and entered her in a head start program through the school system. The head start program alone ended up being a nightmare. The first year went fabulous. The teacher was amazing. The second year was just plain scary. She was only four years old at that time and the teacher that she was given didn't seem to know how to handle children like her. Or better yet, didn't want to. I received calls almost daily asking me to come and pick her up because nothing made her happy. The teacher made some moves that I felt were uncalled for, and then Brianna started reacting. She would head bang until her head bled and scream at the top of her lungs in an attempt to stay out of school. From a child that is extremely loving and had never banged her head that way before, this was a scary change. Even the daycare she was dropped off at after school starting making some worrisome claims.

I made the decision to pull her out of the program. I still feel like I made the best decision. Brianna stopped head banging and went back to being a loving and caring child. I met another parent during one of Brianna's speech therapy sessions that was talking about having to pull her son from a program at school. Scary enough, it was from the same program I pulled Brianna from. I do voice this opinion very loudly. IF any parent ever feels uncomfortable or your child, whether verbal or nonverbal, shows any signs of distress, then something is wrong and it's obviously an unhealthy place for your child to be. Never let anyone make you feel like your decisions are the wrong ones. Only a parent/caregiver knows their child best. I let others in the school convince me a couple of times that everything was fine and I'll never forgive myself for that.

Brianna started kindergarten at a different school not long afterward, and at eight years-old, she still remains there with the same exact teacher. Brianna absolutely adores her. Summer time is rough because she'll bring me her back pack to indicate it's time for school. Do we still head bang? Sure. She never lost that habit completely once she picked it up. She's still a typical child with some typical tantrums from time to time but they are nowhere near the velocity they were back during those earlier days and the meltdowns are fewer and far between. She may not have been able to speak during those times in her life, but she was able to speak volumes in her actions and gestures. And in that retrospect, she was communicating her feelings to the max.

She now takes speech and occupational therapy at her elementary school. She also sees several doctors on a regular basis: Child Development Clinic, Cancer Clinic (for thalasemia beta), eye doctor, pediatric dentistry, psychologist, etc. As of this date, she has not been put on any medications stronger than a vitamin.

I have done tons of research and reading about the certain vitamins and diets that are miracle cures for Autism. We have actually tried several of these, everything from the GFCF diet (gluten free/casein free), probiotics, Omega 3's, the list goes on. The GFCF diet didn't do much for Brianna but I have heard wonderful things from other parents so it's always worth a try. The vitamins, however, do seem to help, at least in the aspect of her health. Brianna has always had stomach issues so the probiotics keep her on track and help her system to work properly. I haven't seen enough change from the other ones to praise them, but we do try the ones the doctors suggest. I'm comforted to know that the multivitamins help her body in the aspect of nutrients and improving her overall health.

I could honestly write a book alone on the many homeopathic remedies for Autism and some of the suggested procedures that some parents are now giving a go. We have tried a few, but most of them are vitamins or diet related. There are some procedures I would never try on Brianna out of fear. Some are outlandish. My rule of thumb: if it seems dangerous, it most likely is and, therefore, I'm not going to jump on that bandwagon.

So far our best successes have been from therapy and school. She also loves the iPad programs now out for Autism, and she really responds to a lot of them. One on one interaction has also helped her improve and learn.

I best describe this aspect of our life as one huge maze. We start at the beginning and make our way through. If we come to a wall of fire so to speak (therapies or suggested 'cures' that seem wrong), we are obviously going to turn around. We will keep trudging along to the next part of the maze until we find the finish line. There is no quitting. That is not an option.

During the writing process of this book, Brianna attended a camp for Autistic children. What they were able to accomplish with her just by doing fun outdoor activities was amazing! Another diagnosis was suggested to us by a doctor while we were there, and we are currently scheduled to go through the Genetics clinic again in the following months to see what will come of this particular path. Please keep Brianna in your prayers as we travel yet another path in the next few months.

Chapter 12

The Golden Ticket

I always loved the part of the movie, *Charlie and The Chocolate Factory*, when the chocolate bars are opened and the golden ticket is found hidden inside. Excitement runs rampant among the children as they discover they will be the ones that enter the gates into Willy Wonka's Chocolate Factory. When I began writing this book and coming up with my outline, this chapter heading popped into my head. I realize most of the things that you have read thus far about Autism seem negative. There are a lot of hardships involved with this diagnosis. But there are also a lot of positives that occur along the way. I like to dub them our golden tickets, those tickets that allow us to move forward in our everyday lives.

Our first ticket occurred not long after Brianna was diagnosed and she started school and speech therapy. We went through what seemed like several long and agonizing months of repeatedly mimicking objects that we wanted Brianna to ask for. These objects might be a favorite toy or a food item that she would pull me to or point at. She had me trained to follow her when she grabbed my hand or pointed her finger. The speech therapist reprimanded me, and she had every right to.

"Sabrina, you have to let her tell you what she wants. No matter how hard it will be for you not to follow her signals, have her ask."

So I did, and boy was it hard. Brianna started having meltdowns immediately. She could not understand why mommy suddenly stopped responding to all her gestures. She seemed to know the words but she either didn't want to say them or her brain kept getting stuck on overdrive with incoming information and she couldn't get her thoughts moving forward and out.

Meltdowns are an understatement for the tantrums she threw. She just couldn't understand why mommy wouldn't just get the object she was furiously pointing too. In fact, I can pretty much compare this to when Helen Keller was going through her training with her tutor. She was wild and unpredictable. But finally one day, she *did it*. She looked at me with those big blue eyes and said "Juice". It was a very emotional moment. We still use one word commands for a lot of things and even a sentence or two here and there but she mostly sticks to her sounds and the copycat game. From time to time though, she'll surprise me by saying something new and out of the blue. Those are the golden tickets that I look forward to the most.

Other tickets have followed. Other goals like eating with a fork, picking up after herself, putting her shoes on, and other tasks are golden moments that make it on that wonderful list. In fact, just a couple of days ago while writing this very book, Brianna awarded us with a couple more golden tickets to add to our collection.

Brianna has just returned from summer camp a couple of weeks ago, a wonderful camp specifically for children on the spectrum. I was terrified. Aside from grandparents, Brianna has never been away from me more than a couple of nights at most and here she would be gone for an entire week. She's non-verbal so you can imagine all the nightmares that presented themselves to me as I packed her up for her camping adventure. Friends have raved about how wonderful the camp is and how amazing they are with the children. I caved and gave in, and with a really huge push (it took a lot of pushing) from family and friends, I registered her for her week long getaway.

The results were amazing. She had a wonderful time and came home calmer and even happier. When we went to pick her up from the camp, they presented us with the work she had done and a group picture of her and her cabin mates and counselors. I took the picture and placed it on my desk at home until able to procure a frame to hang it in her room. Brianna came through the kitchen and looked toward the desk, headed toward it, and picked up the picture. I happened to be sitting at my desk getting a little work done so I was fascinated. I watched her as she gazed at the picture. She stared at it for a few minutes before looking up at me. Yes, she looked up at me and met my gaze!

"Friends?" she asked.

My breath caught. Did I just hear her right?

"Friends?" she asked again.

Lord, I didn't hear her wrong. Tears threatened.

I grabbed her arm. "What's that, Brianna?" I asked.

I knew what she had said, but I hoped that she would say it one more time.

She looked at the picture again. "Friends?" she asked.

At this point, I was really emotional.

I nodded and gave her a hug. "Yes, Bri, those are your friends. You will see them again next summer at camp." How could she know that one word was worth a hundred golden tickets?

You never know when you are going to find one, when that chocolate bar will be the one that holds the screams of joy and tears of happiness. I can tell you though, that golden ticket is worth more to me than all the gold in the world. Screw the gold at the end of the rainbow, give me a chocolate bar with a golden ticket any day!

Chapter 13

Sibling Shout out!

How can I possibly write this book without giving a shout out to my other two beautiful children? Brianna is my oldest at eight years-old. I have two that followed behind her. Charlie is seven years-old, and then Addy came along a few years later. She is two. She was my surprise. I really had no big plans to have any more children but the good Lord had other ideas, and truthfully, I'm glad he did. Although I will now declare openly that my days of having children are over, I don't know what I would do without my small crew. They are my world.

I've often been asked what it must be like to be a sister or brother to a special needs child. What differences their life must carry as a result and what responsibilities for the future will they have to hold. I can't answer the first question since I'm not in their shoes. Does it bother me? I would be lying if I said it didn't. Charlie and Addy are my rock. They help me balance life in our crazy world, and I know that when the time comes, they will hold a huge responsibility that most children never have to worry about.

The situation reminds me of that movie, *The Rain Man*. It's one of those movies that you can't help but tune into. It's timeless. But I have to admit that it's hard to watch the interaction between Dustin Hoffman and Tom Cruise and not get emotional.

In my younger years, I distanced myself from that. I could watch the movie and walk away feeling sympathetic for the characters and for the families portrayed. Never in a million years did I know I would be the mother to a special needs child. It's not something that's planned, it just happens. I was one of those that would see a family dealing with it, smile with sympathy, and then turn and walk the other way as fast as I could. I'm ashamed of myself for that. If I had known what I know now, I would have headed in their direction, gave them a huge hug, and made a new friend. I'm older now, and way more humbled by my daughter.

I can't tell you how many times I have seen a mother just like myself walking through a grocery store with her hair tumbling down and tired eyes as she scrambles to grab everything she needs as quickly as possible. I remember one mother who had her son in a buggy. He was screaming noises out as fast as she was walking. She looked exhausted. Her little boy was really way too big for the shopping cart but he seemed content to flap his hands as she quickly tossed another item in. He would see something and scream and the mother would look around frantically trying to figure out what was causing his excitement or distress. She had her view of everyone blocked off. You could tell she was only focused on getting the things she needed and find the exit as soon as possible. How could I tell? Because I'm usually that mom with my hair tumbling down, tired eyes, and tunnel vision while my own child who is also too big for the cart sits happily flapping her hands.

I touched the woman's shoulder, and a look of impatience crossed her face. Someone had just interrupted her momentum, and courtesy was probably not on the top of her list at that moment. She looked up, and I smiled. "You're doing a great job," I told her.

I pointed to her son. "He reminds me of my daughter."

Brianna happened not to be with me that day, but I could tell she understood what I meant because the lines on her face smoothed out and her eyes watered.

"Thank you," she whispered before ducking her head to the task at hand and hurrying on.

Some people are genuinely nice and some aren't nice at all. Some claim your child is being too loud or others pull their children to the other side of the aisle and hurry past you hoping you don't follow behind them. I am honestly happy about one thing. My other two children will know kindness. They are being raised in a world very different from others, where meltdowns and flapping hands are the "norm" for us. Charlie will often be the one to speak up when he sees a disgusted or confused stare our way. He will point to his sister and say, "That's my sister. She's Autistic."

I realize that like Tom Cruise's character in the movie, that my children will sometimes have that overwhelmed feeling. They will envy their friends and wish for a normal life, lives where going to the movies isn't an act of congress or where having a friend over can sometimes mean adjusting rooms to accommodate the quiet Brianna needs at night. Most of the friends we have now are either family or have known us for a long time, but I know the time will come when they will meet new ones and their parents will be uneasy having their child stay over because of Brianna. I realize that one day, both Charlie and Addy will hit dating age and they will bring home dates that will meet Brianna for the first time. Growing up is hard enough, and now they will not only have to grow up but adjust their growing up around having a special needs sibling.

So, in all honesty, I can't answer for Addy and Charlie on how they will react to each new situation as it arises. I do know that they love their sister very much, and they have a great understanding that Brianna may or may not always be the way she is. We just don't know whether or not her speech will develop more or if she'll always only be able to use one word commands. Development wise, we just take it day to day and do the best we can.

I can only pray that their love for their sister grows with each day, and that they feel as blessed as I do that God gave us Brianna to watch and care for. I do know that Brianna loves them very much. I often find her stroking Addy's hair when Addy is taking a nap, and I'll often see Brianna and Charlie hugging on the bed watching TV together when they don't know I'm watching. Those are the moments that pull me through each day. Those are the moments where I know they accept their sister for who she is. Those moments are my little piece of Heaven.

Chapter 14

True Love

Being a single parent to a special needs child is never easy. You are playing Mom and Dad all the time. The extra responsibilities, and the late nights can wear anyone out. I give a shout out to all those single parents whether Mom or Dad that does this every day on your own. I've been there, and I know how hard it can be. I've been lucky to have a great support system along the way, and I can't thank my family enough for that.

It's extremely hard to date anyone when you are a single parent to kids, and it's especially hard when that child has a special need. So I just simply didn't date. I would go to work and come home and start that routine all over again the next day. When I first moved home, I stayed with my father and my step-mom for a few months until I was able to secure a place for me and the kids. It was during that time period that I met the man that is still in our lives today. Brianna and Charlie were very small. Charlie was a year old and Brianna two when we met, and it was love at first sight. Well not technically for me, but for my kids. Kevin happened to be good friends with my dad, and the kids took to him quickly.

He was always at the house visiting with my father when the kids and I would arrive home in the afternoons, and the kids would run to him immediately after getting out of the car. He would play with them and show them all the attention they craved. It didn't take too terribly long before he wormed his way into my heart as well. He took special care with Brianna and would never get aggravated with her when she would have trouble communicating. She would dance around him, and he would just laugh.

The kids have formed a special bond with him and that was the part that resulted in me falling in love with him. He had always wanted children and had never had any. That is until today. We now have a two year-old little girl together, but he still claims that his first children were those not of his blood. He doesn't treat any of them differently, and I can't express how much that means to me.

It takes a special person to go from living a very normal life to taking on the tasks and responsibilities that we deal with on a daily basis. He tells me every day that he would never change it for the world. Brianna has found small ways of worming herself into his heart and she has him wrapped.

When we took Brianna for her first year of summer camp at Kamp Kaleidoscope, I was a nervous wreck. Kevin kept comforting me on the way and telling me to be strong.

He said, "Now don't cry, because if she sees you cry, she'll get upset."

I nodded as he helped me and Brianna out of the truck and grabbed her by the hand. We stepped inside and were greeted warmly by the staff and counselors. As I finished getting Brianna checked in, I turned to find Kevin watching her and crying! Yes, crying. What a support system I had with me, but my heart swelled that day. Kevin does not show emotion much. He's a true blue male in that aspect, but that day, he showed how much he thought of her. She can't say "I love you", but she shows him in other ways, and I know that means more to him than anything.

Sometimes you don't need words to create friendships and relationships that last forever. Brianna and Kevin have proved that to me on many occasions when I have witnessed him holding her for the doctor or watching his tears as we rush her to the ER when she's sick and we can't figure out what's wrong. I've watched him rock and hold her as she cries because she doesn't understand why she's so sick, when her fever has climbed dangerously high.

We are like any other normal couple. We have habits that get on each other's nerves, and we have our arguments. We have almost nothing in common. He's a workaholic country boy that would rather be on a tractor than stuck at home any day, and I'm kind of a city girl, book nerd, that's happiest when my nose is stuck in a book or sitting at home with my kids. But we share one thing in common that cancels all our opposites out: our love for our kids. I couldn't ask for more.

Chapter 15

Trading Places

If you haven't noticed yet, alongside being a mom, I'm also a sap for movies and I'm a huge bookworm. Nothing wrong with either since it's my way of escaping. Nights tend to be "me" time, that peaceful moment when my small crew is safely tucked into bed. In saying this, it was actually one of those shows on TV that helped me come up with this entry.

Reality shows are trending these days, in every shape and form. It's almost like Hollywood has run out of things to film, and is now turning to human drama. *Trading Places* is where Mom's switch families for a length of time to see how each family lives. Each Mom makes a list for the Mom that's going to replace her. They must go by the other Mom's rules and routines for a week after they have switched homes. I started to giggle.

Why did I find this funny? I imagined myself switching places with one of those moms, and I shook my head. Never in a million years would I imagine myself with another family and their responsibilities. Would that other Mom last more than five minutes in my home once they encounter one of Brianna's first meltdowns? How would they react when Brianna starts doing her happy dance and screaming at the top of her lungs? How would they react when she starts shrieking at bath time due to her fear of the bathtub or her constant gestures as she tries to tell you something while the other two children are yelling "mommy" back to back like it's the only word in the dictionary?

What about me? Would I want to switch places with a parent that has no children with special needs? I thought about this for a minute. I kept imagining myself not having to worry about when the best time to go to the store with as few meltdowns as possible will be or how I'm going to get Brianna's newest container down from the highest perch near the ceiling she managed to throw it to.

No, I rather like my life. I love those moments when Brianna comes behind me and gives me the biggest bear hug with Addy and Charlie not far behind. I love being Brianna's biggest hero as I try my hand at playing spider man. Those containers will break my back one day! I love the bursts of giggles that escapes Bri's lips as she finds something in the room humorous and only she is privy to the secret. I love the smile that spreads across my face as the giggles become infectious and my other two children join in.

No, I'd never switch places. I'm meant to be right here, right here to start that game of tickle monster, turning the laughs into squeals. I'm meant to be here to rock Brianna when she's hurting and there are no words to tell me where the pain is coming from, right here to tackle those questions my kids bring home when they are trying to understand why someone asks them why their sister is so weird. Right here where I'm surrounded with the best hugs and best kisses the world can offer. Yes, I believe that I'm very proud to be here.

Chapter 16

Who Needs Words?

I wish that I could offer this book in Brianna's words, her feelings and emotions instead of mine. I wish I had the right words to explain the things that Brianna's mind sees every day. How does she see the world? I can only make guesses as I watch her face. I can only imagine what she sees when she starts to giggle. What causes the spontaneous laughter? I can only make guesses as to what her mind sees when she cries, tears rushing down her face. What caused the upset? What caused her such extreme sadness? The answer is never apparent.

I know that from reading and watching movies such as *Temple Grandin* that her mind works in a whole different capacity than ours. She sees things in a whole different light. For example, what we see as a simple house fly may look like a huge monster to her. If I were given one wish, I would wish for a peek inside Brianna's head, just long enough to see what she sees, to see if I could find the key to unlocking her words.

I couldn't imagine living in a world I couldn't speak in. My daddy would say that world would be impossible for me. He'd joke that a bar of soap couldn't shut me up. I'm a shy person by nature but I *love* to talk. I love to tell stories and share everything I've done during my day. I love talking about what I'm reading or what funny thing my child did. What must it be like not to be able to say those things?

In that aspect, I can't blame Brianna for her meltdowns. I get frustrated when I have to repeat a sentence more than once when asked a question. I couldn't imagine how frustrating it must be to want something and not always being able to express what that need is.

Brianna finds other ways to express her needs and feelings aside from words. We do use a word here and there for several things, and even recently, have started using a couple of words together. She gestures and pulls me to the places she wants me to be. She even uses her noises as ways of communication from time to time and I've picked up on some of that secret language. My selfish heart wants her to be able to come home and tell me about her day and to sit in my lap and have conversations a mother and an eight year-old little girl should have.

I was once asked in an IEP meeting what I would like to see from Brianna in her list of goals. It was her very first IEP meeting I had ever attended, and she was so little. I remember looking up and saying, "As bad and selfish as this may sound, I would love for her to look at me and say, 'mommy, I love you.'" I have come to realize over the years that I don't need those words from my daughter. She shows me in all kinds of ways her love for me. Her hugs and kisses hold more than a million words at a time. I know she loves me. I see it in her eyes everyday when she looks at me.

While writing this book, Brianna had one of the worst meltdowns I have ever encountered. It was horrific the tears and screams that came from that beautiful little girl. I wrapped my arms around her as she lay in the bed, and I watched as she picked up my hand and laid it upon her forehead. I rubbed the spot she indicated and my heart constricted at the whimpers that came out of her mouth. No words, just whimpers. I knew her head hurt. I gave her some Tylenol and climbed back in the bed. We rocked for a couple of hours as I rubbed her head. I leaned over and kissed her forehead and talked to her in whispers telling her how much I loved her. The tears on her face broke my heart, but her cries softened. Her gaze met mine and we stared at each other for a few minutes and you know what happened? She said, "I love you."

This is where my own words evade me because I don't know if I could ever put enough words on this page to describe the way my heart felt at that very moment as I wiped the remaining tears off her small face. A smile inched its way in place of the tears. To Brianna, mommy had just taken her pain away. To me, fields of flowers exploded everywhere, the Heavens poured forth, and all the gold at the end of each rainbow could not have replaced those three words. Is that the first time she's ever said them. No. She has repeated them when asked, but this was the first time she's done it without being prompted, and the look in her eyes was so pure, so innocent.

My work as her mommy will never be done. I will continue to help her grow with each and every day and hopefully even help some of those words continue to flow. I can only hope that she will one day be able to communicate in the ways I know she wants to. For now, I'm happy with each new milestone, and I rejoice in the small moments. I made that statement in her IEP meeting when she was only three years-old in a head start program. She is eight years-old now. It took five years to hear those three words without prompting. Five years, and the moment could not prepare me for the emotions that hit me like a flooding river. Those words will sustain me for years to come. They are the words that tell me that no matter how small I feel, no matter how many times I feel like I fail, that she has faith in me to help her move forward. She has faith in me to protect her, to love her, to make her pain go away, and I have faith that the good Lord will be with me and give me the strength I need to do everything in my power to carry her through each new task.

This reminds me of a few chapters ago. Faith. That little word goes a very long way. And that "I Love You" gave me the world.

Chapter 17

Growing Pains

What does the future hold for Brianna? That's a question that haunts me day in and day out. It's a question I have absolutely no answer for and that scares me. She's growing up fast on me and I know there are some really big decisions that will come our way in the next few years. Decisions that I know I need to be prepared for but my mind wants to tuck them away.

Brianna is eight years-old now and in just a few short years she will be entering her first steps into womanhood. That all important day when she will start her menstrual cycle. How am I going to handle that? I know that right now with the child-like mindset that Brianna has, that she's not going to understand what's happening to her. She may even hit the floor screaming and crying in sheer fear. What would normally occur between a mother and daughter on this special day will go completely different for us.

We will face doctor visits in the next couple of years to make the bigger decisions like whether we should try and stop her cycles with some form of birth control or a shot. I have friends that are now at that stage where they have had to make those decisions and I can only imagine the emotions that they are going through. I'm emotional just writing about it.

I've been asked before if Brianna stays at the stage she's at, and for some reason does not progress even with therapy and interventions, would we one day have a hysterectomy done on her. I'm not going to answer that question here. Why? Because it's a controversial question for some people and I have even been told of some parents almost divorcing over decisions like that. I do know that it's a question that I will pray heavily over and will think hard and long over. It's heartbreaking to have to think about, and if I think about it long enough, I end up in tears. I can only pray that I make the right decisions when that time comes.

What happens if something happens to you? I worry about this a lot. I know that each year Brianna gets older, so do I. I'm not a spring chicken anymore and Kevin is even older than me. I could perish tomorrow in a car accident or some other way. I just don't know what tomorrow will bring. My family has promised me that they will take good care of my little girl but it's still a terrifying thought. I'm only thirty-two years old and I already have to consider wills, trust funds, and so on in preparation for what may come. Do I have everything in order? I'm an independent writer and Kevin is a welder/farmer. Our salaries alone don't have us fully prepared for what the future may hold but we take it day to day and hope that we will have what's necessary in place before that happens.

With my other two children, I have to worry about all the normal aspects of growing up, dates, prom, graduation, college, and maybe one day marriage and grandkids. With Brianna there are all the added decision making and extra worries that go along with her as she grows each year. I can't say I'm fully prepared. I don't think anyone can be fully prepared emotionally for something like that. I have very high goals for Brianna. We will continue to work really hard to see her progress and we will take each day as it comes and try and be prepared as best we can for the unexpected.

Chapter 18

The Real Heroes

I'm sure that every parent wishes they could take all the credit for all the accomplishments that their child makes. Our chests puff out in pride when we see them do something we taught them. With Brianna, we have had a huge team. A team of people that have brought us along the way, and without them, we would not be where we are today.

These individuals don't always get the recognition that they should, and they work each and every day to help my child grow. They *are* our true heroes. Our Superman, Spiderman, and Batman all rolled into one. Without her teachers, doctors, therapists, coaches, and camp counselors, Brianna would not be who she is today. They have all played such a tremendous role.

I know that Brianna can't put the way she feels into words yet, but I can promise you that she has surely given every one of these special people a hug. Well, maybe not the doctors. You'll have to forgive us for that since all she pictures is a big fat needle when she walks in, but hopefully my smile and thank you lets you know just how much of a difference you made in our life as we walked out of that particular clinic that day.

It takes a special person to be a Special Education teacher. I know I haven't gotten permission to put names so I'll leave them anonymous but it takes a special heart and a certain strength to do what they do each day. They soothe fears, change diapers, push wheelchairs, clean faces, feed their students' minds as best they can with the knowledge they know, and they push their ways into our hearts. My heart overflows when Brianna picks her back pack up each morning and looks behind her and says "school." I am confident that her teachers will take good care of her and show her love as they teach her each new lesson. You are our hero.

To the doctors and nurses that have to answer my frantic phone calls when I don't know what her screams of pain are trying to tell me, I commend you. You put up with this worrisome mom on a monthly basis and deal with my endless questions. Trust me, I ask a lot. I'm sure, secretly, the nurses have a cup of straws that they pull from when they hear that I'm the one on the phone, but still they handle each call like a pro and answer my questions as best they can. You are our hero.

To the family members and friends that we hold close to our heart and are always there for us when we least expect it, we love you. You are there to cheer us on during each milestone, there with a shoulder to cry on, there to make Brianna feel welcome and as normal as she can, and there to hold our hands when we feel so alone. No matter how much a person would like to feel like they can handle any situation on their own, it's not always possible. I can't tell you how many times I have picked up the phone frantically and called my sisters, best friend, and daddy and cried as I became overwhelmed by the day's events. You all hold me up when I need that extra support, and I could not do what I do on a daily basis without my family and friend's support behind me. You are all my light at the end of the tunnel. You are our hero.

To my two beautiful children that are learning to live in this world with a special needs sibling by your side, I love you with all of my heart. No matter how complicated the day gets, you are there to lend a smile and a hug, there to climb in mommy's lap and lay your small heads upon my shoulder, and there to make me laugh when no one else can. You are two of Brianna's biggest supporters and playmates. There is no doubt in my heart, the love she has for the both of you and the love you have for her. You, my beautiful Charlie and Addy, are our hero.

To Kevin who gets to hear me cry the most, the one that holds me each night and talks over our fears for the coming years, the one who holds my hand as we await each new bit of news, the one who laughs with me when I share a funny story, and the one that holds a special place in the mine and the kids heart, you are our hero.

To all the other beautiful and wonderful people that we have had the pleasure of meeting along the way, we thank you. To all the therapists that have had a hand in Brianna's learning process, to the coaches that have helped her succeed with a new goal, to the camp counselors that work with her in the summer, to the random people that stop by and offer a hand and a smile, we love and appreciate you all. You are our hero.

To the good Lord above who listens to my endless prayers and forgives me when I cry out with hate during times of self pity. You are our rock and our foundation and I could not imagine this journey without your love to guide our way. You are our Heavenly father and our hero.

To my daughter, Brianna who teaches me everyday a little more about her world, who shows me that we can endure each day with a giggle fest and lots of snuggling sessions. You have taught me how to be patient, humble, and caring. You have brought out the humor in me and taught me how to laugh at the small things in this world. You have taught us that sometimes a good laugh is the best medicine and wrestling matches with your brother are the best thing ever. You are my hero and we would not be who we are without you. You make us better just by being in our lives. You are our hero.

Here is a big thank you to all the heroes in our life. Our life has been enriched twice as much just by your presence. We love you all!

Chapter 19

Confessional

I decided to put this chapter in at the last minute. I wanted a chapter for people to be able to confront me with questions about being a parent to a child with Autism and to share their opinions and feelings. I put some feelers out there and got this response. Unless a person indicated they wanted their identity known, I left their identity anonymous:

When kids see my students at school some will say "What's wrong with him or her?" I say (maybe I'm not supposed to at school). God made them special and He loves them very much and so should we. My question has always been about raising "normal" siblings and their discipline. In the cases of one not being disciplined for things your "norms" are and how you explain it's acceptable with one but not the "norms". I often wonder how difficult that is especially when the "norms" are younger. Seems like a very difficult situation with one things are gray but with the "norms" things are black and white. Right or wrong.

I love difficult questions and this one above is a really tough one. Why? We battle this each and every day. Charlie is only eighteen months younger than Brianna so he questions everything that we have to discipline him on. I mean everything. If he gets in trouble for talking too much in class, then he asks us why Brianna doesn't get the same kind of sad notes home. If he's punished for talking in a situation where silence is a must, such as a sermon at church or a speaking engagement, he asks why Brianna isn't punished when she makes noises all the time. We have to sit down with him with each individual obstacle and explain to him that there are some situations where there are differences between the two of them that call for different measures. As he grows, I can tell that he's slowly starting to understand those differences and the battles aren't quite as fierce and the questions not so often.

I will admit that I'm not the perfect parent. I make mistakes every day. And there are incidents where really both children should get in trouble. Brianna knows when she's done wrong and I know that she can still get a time out. There are times when I may get on to Charlie and not Brianna. I do not mean to do this and I find myself feeling horrible about it afterwards. I have to constantly remind myself that there are times when punishment is acceptable for both. As Addy gets older, we are beginning to face the same arguments that we faced with Charlie and I know that these will continue as they grow. I don't think there is a good answer for this question. I can say that I hope that we make the right decisions but I know that it will be a problem that we will continue to face each and every day of their childhood. I can only pray that we handle it wisely and make the right choices.

Here's something from a mother with a son with Autism. Her frustrations about outside involvement and questions:

When someone asks why I spoon fed my 5 yr old because they felt he should have been doing it on his own. Then you try your calmest best to explain why, not that it's their business, and they have the begonias to say that

Autism is just all in my head as an excuse to keep my kid little. Angry much? Yes, yes I was.

Have I had similar situations happen to me? Constantly. Why? Most children with Autism look and appear completely normal outwardly so most people just expect them to be as normal as you and me. In fact, this situation happened just last week. On my way back from taking Brianna to a check up with her ear doctor, we stopped by briefly at the store to grab a few things on our way home. The cashier watched Brianna curiously as she twirled a watering can in her hand and started flapping her hands as she jumped up and down squealing. Thankfully this cashier was very polite and when she looked at me with questioning eyes, I explained to her that Brianna had Autism. Her response: "Oh wow, really, she looks so normal. I would have never guessed!" I'm just happy that she responded in such a positive manner when a lot of times we get ugly remarks like, "You need to spank that child!" "Momma, that girl is strange!" "Will you look at her?" "I wonder why her mom is letting her do that." "That's just so weird!" It happens all the time and I realize that this is a situation we will have to face from now on.

Feelings from another mother with a child with special needs:

Some people truly want to understand, but others ask questions with a judgment already waiting to come out. Those are the people I can't stand to be around.

The world is faced with prejudice. There really is no way to get away from it and when you are in a category that people like to direct that prejudice, you are bound to be exposed to it on a daily basis. The truth is people are scared of what they don't understand. And sometimes fear can turn into hate and disgust. Those people are the ones that often like to taunt and yell 'retard' from across the room. It's a shame really that we aren't always educated to those with special needs, and as a result of that lack of education, these children and adults now have to face the ridicule that comes with that ignorance. Peer pressure and bullying play into that very category. It's a scary game, and I worry constantly when news reports deliver a new headline about an individual with special needs or learning disabilities being abused, raped, or killed. I guess that's where my momma bear protectiveness comes into play. Brianna can't speak to tell me she's been bullied, so therefore I find myself constantly on alert to anyone and everyone that may pass judgment on us before ever getting to know us.

Like stated above, we run into people every day that have automatically passed judgment prematurely. They either don't want to know that Brianna has Autism or they just don't care. Like the mother in the earlier statement, people can just be plain cruel with some of the things they may direct or yell out. But on a positive note, we must not forget that there are just as many caring and nice people in the world as there are ugly. We remember the ugly the most because it hurts and stings no matter how hard your exterior may appear. To those that do ask questions and give their support, I thank them from the bottom of my heart.

From a grandparent of a special needs child:

Oh Sabrina I love this. We were once at a restaurant and a little boy pointed at Benjamin and said to his mother, "his eyes look funny." Of course the mother swatted at the little boy and whispered for him to hush. I think this is what we were all taught to do, whisper like a disability is shameful. I love that you are writing your book so that we all have a voice. After that evening, I developed my response for children, we are all different, you and I are different but we are all wonderfully made by God. To us, Benjamin is perfect!

Not much to say in regard to this statement except that I couldn't agree more! To me Brianna is perfect and these children and special adults are God's special angels.

One from a fellow parent:

Are there things in every day conversation that offend you without you really meaning for it to or you just can't help it, that little cringe when something is said that the other person may have not even realized it was offensive to you as a mother of a special needs child?

Yes, this has happened to me and still does on occasion. I have to remember that not all people live our life and I have to remind myself that what they may find different or even repulsive may be normal for us. I've had conversations with people before that didn't know I had a child with special needs. A person or an individual walks by that does have one and the person I'm talking to makes a comment and then laughs. They turn back to me and find that I'm not smiling at all. In fact, I'm frowning. I explain to them that I have a child that is different and their face gets red. Here's the thing though, not all of those people are being ugly on purpose. They have been taught that it's normal. I remember being in high school and laughing as someone pointed out something about someone. Did I want to laugh? No, I wanted to fit in so therefore I did. Am I proud of it? No, but all I can do now is change it as I get older and educate my own children that that behavior isn't acceptable. You would be surprised at how many people don't technically want to make fun or laugh. They were taught that it was acceptable behavior and sometimes all that needs is for one person to stand up and say that's not cool, to change the rules.

I also run into those that love to give free advice . . . a lot. This is not to say that I don't mind getting friendly suggestions on how to change this or do that. But there is a limit that even a parent of a normal child can find overwhelming. When someone starts to give advice to the brink of exhaustion where the suggestions become absurd, I do find myself getting offended. But I once again have to remind myself that some of those people are genuinely interested in helping and others merely suggest it just to get a glimpse into a world that astounds them.

My rule of thumb is to take it with stride. I normally smile and nod and walk away with all parties happy, but that rule stops at comments or advice that turns rude or just plain mean. Then I allow myself to find my voice. I will give anyone the benefit of the doubt. Curiosity can harbor some very strange questions from people. I can generally tell which comment or question is offensive or just someone being helpful or curious.

From an interested person:

At one time I wanted to be a Special Ed teacher. I so look forward to reading your book! When Bri has a long crying time, does she let you hold her? Does she talk?

In answer to the first question, yes, she does let me hold her the majority of the time. We have several different types of crying spells so it's all according to the type that we are having. If she's sick and crying, she will almost always let me cuddle with her and rock her. When's she's over stimulated, she doesn't always let me hold her and in some circumstances, she swings around and fights so much, I would rather not hold her in those situations. At that point, I normally wait until the right time to approach her. She will often approach me first and hug me to let me know in her own quiet way. When we are having a flat out tantrum due to an object she may want that someone else has or something else, I choose not to go to her then because I have found that if I do, she thinks that she has won the right to go and steal that person's toy, food, or other object. The majority of the time, however, she will allow me to hold her.

In answer to the second question, yes and no, according to what she has progressed to over the years. She can use simple commands like chips, drink, juice, go stinky, hurt, and so on. The last couple of years she has even put together three words at a time such as "I go outside." For the most part though, she makes noises and uses gestures to communicate. She has come a long way the last few years from where's she's at on using words. It's my hope that she continues to progress and use even more words in the next few years.

I want to thank each and every one of you that contributed to this chapter. I appreciate your input more than you could ever know.

Chapter 20

Just Call Me Sgt. Mom

I sat around for a long time trying to come up with a title for this book. Then one night while sleeping, I woke up with a start and it was there. As I've put my words to paper, I keep thinking back to the title above and I ask myself: Why this title? Why refer to myself as Sgt. Mom? I'm nowhere near military standards. I would know because I was once married to a Sergeant in the Marine Corps.

My clothes are usually wrinkled from holding kids. I couldn't even begin to tell you where my iron is when my dryer seems to do the job just fine. I'm mostly disorganized as much as I hate to admit that. My outfits are always accentuated by stains from little fingers. My sense of humor usually involves a story about a diaper and a baby's bottom. My idea of a vacation is a good nap and maybe a movie without the kids. Most people would consider themselves lucky if they actually see me at the store completely dressed meaning that I at least have make up on, appropriate clothing, and my hair is fixed. The majority of the time, I'm missing one of the three … well in clothing, I do not refer to being nude, but having on jeans instead of pajama bottoms.

I'm nowhere near perfect and I don't claim to be. Are any of us parents really perfect? There may be a few that want to think so but we all have our quirks and our imperfections and I'm okay with that. That makes me realize that none of us are really the "norm". What is normal anyway? Don't we all have something odd about us? I know that I have my oddities. I'll even declare some of them publicly. I love to have cleaning lists.

Although I don't follow half of them, I make them out all day long. I have a thing for Elvis and old movies. Move over modern Hollywood! I like to dance around the house and sing at the top of my lungs when no one's looking. I love fresh sheets on the bed even going so far as changing them daily which drives Kevin insane and does not help our water bill. I hate making phone calls, so much so that I sometimes bribe my twin sister to make them for me and pretend to be me. Yes, I'm admitting this. The list could go on.

We all have our pet peeves and our little idiosyncrasies and that's okay because that makes us who we are. Children with Autism and other special needs just have more than the usual or seem to because they look at the world in a different light and outwardly show their differences more than the average Joe. But really, aren't we all in some way Autistic? Don't we all have some kind of strange habit hiding in our closet? Maybe someone you know likes to do something weird like collect string in different colors and sort them out. That would be considered an Autistic tendency.

For now though, I'll continue to share Brianna's story and tell the world about her life in hopes of changing the world one mind at a time. I'll never forget one piece of wise advice from my now ten year-old niece at a time that she was standing up for Brianna at school. One little boy pointed at Brianna as she exhibited behavior beyond what is customary and says, "Something's wrong with her." My niece looked at him and said, "Something's wrong with all of us." A statement has never been truer.

I am a mom to three beautiful children. My oldest has Autism and this is our story.

To Be Continued. . .

16445120R00045

Printed in Great Britain
by Amazon